Presented to:

Never Forget The Difference You've Made

Made in the USA
Coppell, TX
06 December 2021

67300014R00066